Cows in the Living Room:

Developing an Effective Strategic Plan

and Sustaining It

By

Major General Robert Mixon
Major General John Batiste
Partners, Level Five Associates, LLC
U. S. Army (retired)

Copyright 2014 Level Five Associates
All Rights Reserved
ISBN-13: 978-1503066878
ISBN-13: 1503066878

Cover design & illustrations © 2014 Mark Gerber, Gerber Studio

(www.gerberstudio.com)

"John Batiste and Robert Mixon are well versed in the theory and practice of leadership, to include the value of strategic planning to provide clarity and focus. Collectively, they have over eight decades of leadership experience, to include 16 years in corporate America. They speak with authority gained from experience honed on the battlefield and board room.

With their strategic planning process and techniques, they will assist you to improve your profit margin and run circles around your competition. I fully endorse their work to build cultures of performance characterized by decentralization and empowerment."

    ~ General Barry R. McCaffrey, US Army (Ret.)

Acknowledgement

The authors attribute their strategic planning expertise to decades of study and practical experience in the US Military, followed by application in private companies. We specifically acknowledge CDS Monarch and Klein Steel Service Inc in Rochester, New York. The roadmap and the strategic process were two essential elements of the CDS Monarch model.

Introduction

There was once a young farmer, who wanted to find a wife, so he went into a nearby village and successfully courted a woman, married her, and brought her to her new home on the farm. They began their new life together raising dairy cows. As winter began, one day the wife came in and found that all of the cows were in the living room. Astonished, she asked why. Her husband replied, "It's winter, and the barn has no heat. Since we depend on these cows for our living, they need to be inside." Slowly, she became more and more accustomed to having the cows indoors. Then, after a few months, a neighbor from her village came over to see how she was doing. When she came into the living room, she was shocked to find the dairy cows there, calmly standing around. "What are you doing with cows in your living room?" she blurted out, to which the wife replied, "What cows?"

This book is about cows – the cows in your living room. Just as the wife became so accustomed to having cows she no longer realized were indoors, so do leaders of most companies and organizations. They don't realize that they have become satisfied with being "good enough." Content to leave the cows alone, they just accept the status quo. Without an effective strategic plan, "cows" will become right at home in "your" living room.

What you'll find in the pages that follow is a plain, simple formula for building a workable strategy to change your company for good. Equipped with the right strategic framework, you will see how to identify a plan for nurturing cows throughout the seasons – without having to bring them indoors to keep your business healthy. Your "farm" will grow and prosper, and you and your team will be much happier, working in a company that knows how to build a professional organization that anticipates and manages change for the better.

What you'll find in the following pages are our proven techniques to develop a clear mission, vision/intent, and values-based strategic plan that your teammates will understand and adopt. No one will even consider bringing the cows inside for the winter. Enjoy the journey!

Table of Contents

So What Do We Do With Our "Cows"?	**11**
Companies Who Ignore Their Sacred Cows	12
Three Pillars of an Effective Strategy	14
The Origins of the Commander's Intent	15
Establishing a Culture with Core Values	17
Building the Plan of Action	**19**
Why Companies Don't Plan for the Future	19
Time for Real Leadership!	21
The Importance of Assumptions and Trends	21
Team Buy-In at the Senior Levels	22
Getting an Outside Set of Eyes	23
Another Option: Key Result Areas	25
Building the Strategic Roadmap	27
How to Heat the Barn	**29**
Setting the Agenda: The Strategic Planning Session	29
Conducting the Strategic Planning Session	30
Next Steps After the Strategy Session Ends	33
This is a Marathon, Not a Sprint	34
Complacency Can Be Fatal	35
Keep the Cows Healthy and Content All Year Round	**36**
Discipline and Experience Unleash Potential	36
Thoughts on Farming	**42**
The Numbers Don't Lie	42
About the Authors	**46**

So What Do We Do With Our "Cows"?

Like the dairy farmer, every company or organization has "cows". Literally, these "sacred cows" are the core elements of your business – proprietary technology, intellectual property, financial strength, strong performers and leaders, reputation – **_all the qualities which separate you in the marketplace and keep your competitors in your rear view mirror_**. These essential elements are your "milk producers"; you have to keep them safe, healthy, and performing at their best. If you don't nurture them, they wither and die. So does your company.

The problem is -- most senior executives don't pay attention to what matters most. As long as there is no bad news or impending crisis at hand, most feel no need to do much more than "shepherd duty". You've seen this tendency in your profession or field -- as long as the herd are not showing outward signs of illness, most corporate leadership teams operate as though all they need to do is provide support, maintain the milking equipment, conduct regular manure management, and cash the checks coming in.

At those times when bad things *do* happen, these caretaker leaders just manage the wake and ride out the storm. Usually there is someone who can be found to blame, so one standard course of action in crisis management is to find them, then fire them. Next, they'd control the damage by publishing a corporate statement on what steps are being made to investigate the matter, hunker down, wait for time to pass, then resume "business as usual".

We've all seen this behavior demonstrated by senior leaders and their management teams, and the culture of their organization reflects that behavior. Since everything revolves around "business as usual until the wheels come off", few, if any, of the sacred cows are protected or nurtured. When the inevitable crisis comes, any or all of them are at risk. The top performers are insecure, no one owns the outcomes. There's no plan of action. Just a culture of reaction.

Companies Who Ignore Their Sacred Cows

The harsh reality is: <u>After only three years, only 56% of all startup businesses are still in business</u>. Why? Among the leading reasons for failure:

- A. Lack of a clear focus (an effective strategic framework).
- B. Lack of market awareness.
- C. Pride (read hubris).
- D. Optimism versus discipline.

Perhaps equally troubling is the fact that many more companies fail <u>after</u> making it to their 3-year anniversary -- **71%** are gone by year 10 -- for much of the same reasons. It's clear that ultimately most companies reach the tipping point where the sacred cows are no longer safe – unless their leaders establish and sustain a protective framework.

The Framework for Survival and Growth: Strategic Planning

If you are going to build an enduring, resilient organization, then you've got to dedicate yourself and your leadership to building and sustaining that operating system. You may have the most creative, innovative intellectual property since the internet and a tremendous team of professionals with talent, drive, and imagination. Together you achieve a number of successes, weather a few storms. But the evidence indicates that initial success is fragile at best. Very few companies can survive on their last great idea.

The foundation of your system for enduring success lies in building a **strategic planning framework** that works – a **plan of action you and your team establish and share ownership of.** It's not just a written plan; it is a living, breathing document which serves as the foundation of your business life. Your strategic plan captures the culture of your organization and your direction, with measurable outcomes that indicate real progress toward your goals. The strategic plan also serves as the blueprint of your business model, and provides you with an effective engine for making key decisions.

The strategic plan is captured in the first of the Big Six Leadership Principles we call "Set the Azimuth". A Level Five Leader understands the importance of "setting the azimuth" to ensure that an organization has a clear path to success. The leader is responsible for setting a sense of urgency with unambiguous focus and priorities. The vehicle to make this happen is strategic planning, which creates a living roadmap for an organization. The old saying "if you don't know where you are going, any road will get you there" is a recipe for failure.

That said, the last thing you want to do is develop a plan and stick to it no matter what. Remember the old adage about the definition of insanity: "doing the same thing over and over and expecting a different outcome each time." Your strategy will always have an "as of ____" date. Structure, flexibility, and a wide field of view are all key components of the strategic framework. Your strategic planning system is a *living* process. You must keep it off the shelf and on your desk so it remains relevant.

Three Pillars of an Effective Strategy

What drives an effective, viable strategic plan? There are three pillars of an effective strategy: **Mission, Vision (Intent), and Core Values**. These 3 pillars serve as the touchstones, the foundation upon which your strategy is built. Let's examine each pillar.

<u>Mission</u>: *The Mission Statement defines your purpose for existing in the first place.* Your company or organization is rudderless without a clear, concise mission statement. Yet, many companies don't have one – or one anybody can remember or even locate. And, if they do have a mission, oftentimes it has no purpose other than frame filler for wall posters in the executive offices. Your mission should lay out what you do -- whether it is to make products, build things, serve others, create ideas, or some other function. And it should capture how well you do it -- hopefully better than anyone else does.

Vision – the Commander's Intent: *The Vision Statement defines where you are going.* The vision gives direction to your company. One of the best vision statements of the commander's intent ever written was created by President John F. Kennedy in 1963, when he said: "We will send a man to the moon and return him safely by the end of this decade." Hard to misunderstand that vision, and so it is not all that surprising (albeit still amazing) that we achieved that objective. The vision was unmistakably clear; millions of people understood and followed it. In 1969, we achieved that incredible goal of placing a man on the moon and returning him safely. The elegance was in the simplicity of JFK's vision statement, and it translated into outcomes.

The Origins of the Commander's Intent

In the military, however, we have translated *Vision* into the *Commander's Intent*. This is because the concept of the intent has more relevance and importance than vision in many respects. The Army's primary doctrinal publication, FM 3.0, defines the Commander's Intent as:

"…..a clear, concise statement of what the force must do and the conditions the force must establish with respect to the enemy, terrain, and civil considerations that represent the desired end state."

The *Commander's Intent* defines success, then, with a measurable degree of clarity. When everyone knows what the boss wants to happen, they have a shared understanding and focus. They can act individually or as members of a team with what we call "a bias for action." In the absence of other orders or guidance, everyone on your team will know what you want to happen as the desired outcome, and they will move toward those goals. Ideally, your team members will move without being told to do so and embrace the notion that "it is better to ask for forgiveness than permission".

One classic example of the effective use of the Commander's Intent occurred in the Napoleonic Wars. Napoleon Bonaparte had created a huge army by the early 1800s. His 300,000-man Grande Armee' was more than 60 miles wide and 50 miles long when on the march, and controlling it from a horse drawn carriage was virtually impossible. Napoleon solved the problem by creating several corps of approximately 30,000 Soldiers each, and placing a Marshal in command of each one.

Napoleon's Marshals were exceptional battlefield commanders. At the Battle of Jena-Auerstadt in 1806, as well as numerous others in the early 1800s between the French Grande Armee' and the rest of Europe's armies, Napoleon won battle after battle because these Marshals would follow his intent in the absence of orders. He told them, when in doubt: "March to the sound of the guns."

Core Values: Finally, *Core Values define you as an organization*. Somehow, this key element of successful strategic planning seems to get lost in translation. For every Enron Corporation or Bernie Madoff, there are dozens of other (perhaps less notorious) examples of companies and senior executives with no core values. They actively or passively allowed themselves and their team to wander far afield of truth, honesty, and character. Cheating, fraud, theft, corruption –are all products of creating a valueless culture in an organization. Many leaders adamantly deny that they would ever allow these conditions to exist. But no one can deny it happens – over and over.

Establishing a Culture with Core Values

Not only do you have to decide what your core values are, you have to repeatedly state what defines you in terms of values in order to establish a culture where everyone understands and buys in to those core values. As a leader, you have to live them, and insist your teammates do as well, with no tolerance for those who don't. It will not happen automatically; you have to lead the establishment of core values. Our experience has been that there is never too much repetition of the core values. They define you.

The founding principles of your organization must be blatantly obvious to everyone you come in contact with on a daily basis. Meetings, signs, posters, tag lines, greetings, e-mails, letters, business cards – everything reinforces and restates your core values. Many leading companies require their employees to sign a personal commitment statement to the mission/intent/core values on a recurring basis. They are that important.

You must also find and hire new teammates who are hardwired with your stated core values. The truth is that most people do not embrace your values, and you must deliberately assess and evaluate new recruits before you offer them a position on your team. There is a wide variety of on-line assessments and techniques to assist in your recruiting efforts. Your very special core values and culture are key to your success and require the leader's attention. Communicate your values and culture often, and act quickly when one of your teammates steps outside of acceptable behavior. The secret is to attract and retain team members who can flourish within your company's culture.

Once you have set the conditions by establishing a clear ***mission, vision/intent, and core values*** for your organization, you can begin to develop your plan of action -- the strategy that will separate you from your competition, build and keep your edge, and grow your team, every day.

Building the Plan of Action
(So the Cows Don't Have to Come Inside for the Winter)

Knowing who you are, what you do best, and what is sacred to your organization form the basis of your strategic plan; that is, how you intend to be what you say you are. It doesn't happen by chance that you automatically become the leading companies in your field or the best unit in your organization. As Louis Pasteur aptly observed, "Luck favors the prepared mind." You're going to have to <u>earn</u> your place in the market.

Strategic planning forms the structural foundation of your path to get from where you are today to where you want to go in the future. It would seem to be intuitively obvious to devote considerable time, energy, and leadership to building and maintaining this strategy. Yet, most companies do just the opposite – they pay strategic planning lip service at best. Often it is just ignored.

Why Companies Don't Plan for the Future

One reason is that it's <u>hard</u> to focus on strategic planning. Many leaders see the critical work as being the *tactical* work; e.g. doing what must be done right now, today, this week. These leaders are completely immersed in getting product out the door, or completing services by close of business. If they are meeting deadlines and making payroll, things are OK. We often hear comments like: " If I take care of what must be done today and tomorrow, then the long range stuff will take care of itself," or: "I don't need a strategic plan; I just need people to do their jobs every day."

Faced with the reality of meeting customer demands and managing sales and costs on a daily basis, many leaders just lose sight of where they are going in the long run – or how to get there. We see this shortsightedness everywhere, especially with the proliferation of hand held devices to provide us with instant information. Senior leaders can now know virtually every facet of their company's operations, in real time. They can micromanage everything from anywhere – an addictive narcotic! So why plan when you can just monitor and react?

Next time you are in an airport, count the number of people within 50 feet of you who are looking at their hand held devices....versus those who are not. You'll find the numbers extremely one sided in favor of the device addicts. We know a number of senior executives who keep their cell phones beside their beds at night, so they can hear that "ping" when a message or an order comes in at 3:00 AM, then wake up and read it. No wonder so many leaders are sleep deprived tacticians. They not only are completely focused on the here and now, but they are mentally and physically exhausted, too.

Not all that surprising, then, that even the most "sacred" cows end up in the living room for the winter. In the corporate environment we've described in the preceding paragraphs, there's nowhere else for them to go when the first cold snap hits.

Time for Real Leadership!

<u>This is where real strategic leadership comes in</u>. You have to step up and lead the strategic plan in your organization. It is up to you, the person who owns the future direction of your company, to focus the rest of your team on building and maintaining a **values-based, measured-outcomes strategic plan.** You and your team have established the mission, vision/intent, and shared values -- the stage is set to overcome the need to micromanage the present and set free the creative energy of your organization. Now you have to take ownership of the future and develop your strategic plan. You can't do this in the airport or on a hand held device. You have to put that down for a while and assemble your leadership team for some hard thinking, and face to face, frank communication. The good news is it will really pay off, right to the bottom line. And now you'll probably get a lot more sleep in the process.

Where do you start? Good question. Some might answer the first step is to find an offsite location where you can gather up your leadership team for a couple of days so they are separated from the day to day operations. But that's <u>not</u> the first step – the first step is to think about how you want to build the strategy. We call it *thinking through the process*.

The Importance of Assumptions and Trends

Your strategic framework must be based on establishing a current set of <u>assumptions and trends</u>. Think in terms of 2-3 years going forward. Now you're thinking *strategically* instead of tactically. What are the critical assumptions that, if true, you can build your plan upon? Here are some examples of strategic assumptions and trends:

1. The economy will grow at a pace equal to or greater than the past 3 years.
2. Our unions will ratify their contracts when they come up for renewal.
3. Our C-Suite executives will remain in their current positions for the next 3 years.
4. The partnerships we have in place will remain viable during this planning cycle.

These assumptions should be the <u>starting</u> point of your strategic "Roadmap." If they hold true, then the strategic plan you create will be viable. If any of them change, then you should change the strategic plan.

You'll need to circulate these assumptions and trends with your inner circle first, then edit them based on the senior leader inputs and prepare to bring them to your entire leadership team during the strategic planning session. Be conservative in your assumptions up front; that is to say, underestimate the positives and take a lowball approach to what the world around you will look like. Just as the Intel leadership always says, "Only the paranoid survive."

Team Buy In at the Senior Levels

Once you have established the strategic assumptions, it's important to get the leadership to buy in. You'll have to socialize your key leaders to the process, and that will require some focused one-on-one discussions.

Then you'll need to have several executive level meetings a couple of months prior to the actual strategic planning session. Regardless of your specific actions leading into the strategic planning event, you have to insure the buy in work gets done. And you are the only one who can do it initially. No delegating it to the last senior executive who missed one of your meetings. This will send the wrong signal.

Getting an Outside Set of Eyes

Next, you have to ask for and conduct an <u>external evaluation</u> of your organization and your C-Suite leadership, and determine what plan they are currently using. It's possible there really isn't a single plan in place. You may think so, but the external eyes and ears you bring in for this evaluation will give you a more objective view than anything you can do in-house. An outside subject matter expert (SME) team is your best option for this evaluation. Get someone who has "been there and done that" in change management. Experience is extremely important for this objective assessment. There are both surveys and focused interviews this external team should conduct with a number of your leaders, and their feedback will be a critical component of setting the conditions for success of your strategic planning session. Give them your full support right up front.

Plan for a couple of days for this SME team to visit your organization, and for some phone interviews ahead of time. But also insure they conduct face-to-face interviews with your key leadership – C Suite and others that you designate. Be prepared to provide them with a read ahead of your mission, vision/intent, and shared values, as well as your current strategic plan (if you have one) and the assumptions and trends it is based upon. The product of this external evaluation will be an initial SWOT analysis and set of observations you can use to target specific parts of the company you want to sustain –or change. It may also tell you there are some mismatches on your team. That information may drive you to make some personnel moves ahead of the formal strategic planning. Your plan won't work if you don't have the right people -- as Jim Collins says in his book, *Good to Great*, "the right people in the right seat on the right bus."

The final stage of your strategic planning framework is to develop the strategic layout – **The Roadmap**.

Grab This Free Gift!

One of the most popular versions we've used in organizations with autonomous business units is available to you as a *free download from our website*. Simply visit

www.LevelFiveAssociates.com/resources

and you'll find it there.

This Roadmap, when completed during your strategic planning session, will drive the execution of your plan. In this example, the overall strategic focus is on six **Core Strategic Values**:

S1: Provide World Class Service

S2: Develop and Maintain Rewarding Strategic Human Resources Systems

S3 Establish and Exploit Self-Determined Opportunities

S4: Integrate Technology to Optimize Efficiency and Effectiveness

S5: Establish and Maintain Financial Strength

S6: Identify and Maximize Key Strategic Relationships

We'll discuss these Core Strategic Values in much more detail in the upcoming chapters, as they include several key components that, once clearly understood by your leadership team, will help create measurable results. If you develop different ones, they'll certainly serve the same purpose, but we have seen these used with great effect when backed up by determined leadership.

Another Option: Key Result Areas

An alternative model that is applicable to manufacturers, distributors, and companies with a more unified focus or product line involves identifying the list of "must do" objectives that we call "Key Result Areas" (KRAs). These KRAs are key to improving company profitability and usually involve tough, hard to do actions that require dismantling "stovepipes" that are prevalent in too many companies.

The strategic planning team first brainstorms a complete list of KRAs without regard to priority or impact on the company's success. In turn, this list is prioritized and the organization commits to taking on a finite number of the high priority KRAs that can realistically be completed within the next 3 to 6 months with available resources.

The leadership team stands up a Working Group for each KRA and assigns a leader with cross-functional representation from the applicable departments and divisions of the company required to accomplish the task. Generally, these KRAs require significant commitment and require top talent, resources, and support of the leadership team to complete the work. Working Group leader assignments go to up and coming high potential teammates.

The company senior leader team then provides a charter, in writing, to the KRA Working Group to define the objective, resources, and expected timeline for completion.

Another Free Gift!

You can *download a free sample* of the KRA Roadmap by visiting the resources page on our website at

www.LevelFiveAssociates.com/resources

In turn, the Working Group assembles to begin work. Step one is to develop a complete project management action plan in sufficient detail to include ownership, tasks, timeline, and expected outcomes.

Along the way, the senior leader team stays involved with the Working Group with scheduled status reviews. The role of the senior leader team is to fully support, resource, and eliminate obstacles for the Working Group.

The KRA is closed out by the senior leader team when objectives are met and company standard operating procedures are revised to fully capture the new direction established by the completed KRA.

As KRAs are closed out, successes are celebrated with a "Victory List" which sets an expectation for momentum and success. The objective is improved profitability and market share.

As KRAs are closed out, the next priority is moved up in the queue for action. The senior leader team develops a new charter for the next KRA, and the cycle continues.

The list of open KRAs drives strategic planning work and is updated/reviewed every 12 months during annual strategic planning.

Building the Strategic Roadmap

To be able to build the Strategic Roadmap, you have to complete these initial steps prior to the actual strategic planning session:

1. Socialize your senior leadership. Review your Mission, Intent, and Shared Values with them in a face-to-face session well ahead of the SPS.

2. Collectively develop your strategic assumptions/trends.
3. Select, schedule, and conduct a formal external assessment by SMEs for a preliminary SWOT, to include an assessment of your current focus, plan, and leadership.
4. Lay out your Roadmap format, with the Strategic Planning Core Values or agreed upon Key Result Areas.

<u>Now</u> you're almost ready to assemble the team for your two day strategic planning session.

How to Heat the Barn

Your strategy planning session is really the formal development of the organization's way ahead. Like the farmer, you have to plan for winter long before it comes. If you just tend to the tasks at hand, then there's a strong likelihood the cows will be in the living room by winter, because you had no plan to install and maintain a heating system for the barn. The SPS, as we'll call it, forces your entire team to plan for all 4 seasons, even when it may be a delightful spring when you conduct the actual session, and winter seems a long, long way off.

Setting the Agenda for the Strategic Planning Session

As you have no doubt figured out by now, conducting the Strategic Planning Session (SPS) itself is not something you can prepare for the day before the event. And, you still have one final preliminary step remaining. That step is to set and publish the agenda. This blueprint will drive the flow of the session, so it's worth spending a couple of hours in developing it.

Schedule the SPS at least 3 months ahead of the actual dates. Make it clear to your leadership that this is NOT an optional event. Find a site nearby that has conference support capabilities, and establish a contract so they can do the logistics (food, beverages, etc.) Your team should focus on the content of the SPS.

It's also worth considering who attends the formal planning session. You want enough people there to have the kind of quality interaction and contribution that creates outcomes. On the other hand, if you have people attending who haven't been part of the preliminary work, they are probably not going to contribute much to the results. Our advice is to use the *"Two Levels Down Formula." The Two Levels Down Formula = C-Suite + the next level down in your organization.*

Finally, we recommend bringing in at least 2 outside facilitators (external support team) to guide the timeline, take notes, prepare the executive summary, and schedule follow up actions as a result of the SPS. As we have mentioned earlier, experience counts. <u>Your SPS support team should be comprised of leaders and facilitators who have been successful strategic planners and led companies with significant top and bottom line results</u>. This external support team's preliminary work to develop the SWOT (Strengths – Weaknesses – Opportunities – Threats) is key to your success.

Conducting the Strategic Planning Session

Now you should (finally) be ready to go. What follows is a sample of an agenda we have seen used in a number of different companies, all with outstanding results:

<u>Day 1</u>

8:00a – 9:00a	Introduction of the Outside subject matter team, Review of the Mission/Vision (Intent)/Shared Values. Presented by the President/CEO.
9:00a – 10:00a	Establish the Strategic Assumptions and Review the SWOT analysis (3

	year horizon). Presented by the COO or CMO.
10:00a –11:30a	In groups of 5-8 people, review the Strategic Core Values (S1-S6) that will measure company performance/or Key Result Areas (Note the left hand column of Figures 1 and 2). Use a member of the C-suite team to lead each group.
11:30a – 1:30p	Working Lunch with small group tables (insure cross section of staff and leaders at each table). Conduct financial review of company performance during the last hour of the lunch, led by the CFO.
1:30p – 4:00p	Establish and conduct breakout groups to develop strategies for each Business Unit and key staff department. (Or, if applicable, conduct breakout groups with each KRA you identified in the morning). Outside subject matter team circulates to monitor strategy development, as well as C Suite executives.
6:00p – 9:00p	Conduct dinner event, to include guest speaker (outside subject matter expert). Provides opportunity to better understand how leadership enables the strategy to work, build the team, and discuss Day 1 progress.

Day 2

8:00a – 8:30a	Review Day 1 progress. Define outcomes expected. Led by the President/CEO.
8:30a – 11:30a	Small group work continues to develop the S1-S6 specific goals for each business unit and staff element, or KRA. Insure cross functional groups – especially if you are conducting KRA Roadmap development. Both subject matter experts (your external eyes) and C-suite executives circulate and provide input to the development of measurable outcomes as goals for each team.
11:30a – 1:30p	Lunch in small group tables. Conduct guest presentation to highlight a best practice and or success story in the company over the past year.
1:30p – 3:30p	Report by each Business Unit and staff element to entire group. Use key leaders (VPs) of each unit to report on specific plans and outcomes. Budget targets presented and agreed to by C-suite leadership team.
3:30p – 4:30p	Summary provided by outside subject matter team. Timeline set for management plans to be created as outcomes of Roadmap development. Session adjourned.

An important point to remember is: Don't tie yourself to only 2 days as the SPS format. Many companies and organizations find that 2.5 days is preferable –

particularly if you are conducting a major acquisition, a transformation, and/or many of the senior leadership are new to the team.

Next Steps After the Strategy Session Ends

Within 3 business days after your strategic planning session, the outside subject matter experts who facilitated the SPS provide a summary report to the President/CEO, with specific comments and recommendations for approval and distribution to the attendees.

Typically, strategic planning sessions are not recorded. If the company has distributed sites, it might be useful to stream the session so more people can participate. Where possible, though, we recommend bringing the leadership team to one site for face-to-face interaction. The lack of formal recording usually promotes more open discussion, too.

The outside subject matter expert team (SME) will make notes, however, and provide them to the President/CEO in the form of the summary report. As part of the outside subject matter operating agreement, the specific notes of each strategic planning session should always remain confidential, never to be shared with any other organization.

Every quarter going forward, you should conduct quarterly reviews over the succeeding 12 months. The senior leadership should lead each of these Roadmap Reviews (2 hour sessions). During each meeting, the business unit directors or KRA Working Group leaders brief their respective management plan progress with specific metrics indicating success (or lack thereof). Based on these updates, the team modifies selected plans and corresponding portions of the Roadmap if needed.

As you can easily see, now there is a strategic planning **cycle** in effect. You have set a standard of "what right looks like" in your organization for both planning and execution. This is the heart of the process – planning to implementation. Seems very straightforward, but indeed it is more difficult to establish and maintain than it appears to be.   Keep in mind the culture change for a typical organization looking to "turn the battleship" is 2-3 years. That's 3 full SPS cycles.

This is a Marathon, Not a Sprint

Why does the process of change take so long? As we've talked about before, some of it is an intellectual complacency which sets in if you can consistently make payroll. But there are some other reasons, too, which you should be aware of....

We've seen more than a few strategic planning failures, both in the military and the corporate world. The primary reason they fail (and by failure we mean nothing meaningful happens as an outcome of the planning) is because the senior executives essentially took the cows for granted. They assumed everyone will always be productive and satisfied, so when they conducted a strategic planning session, the event was literally just for show. In each instance, the organization became intellectually complacent. No one thinks about winter until it comes. Then, it's too late to heat the barn without crisis managing the whole operation. Crisis management is the antithesis of good strategic planning. It inevitably leads to corporate failure. So if you're not willing to commit to the process for at least 2-3 years – which should create a tradition through repetition and acceptance – don't go down this road.

Complacency Can Be Fatal

Even warfare – the ultimate crucible – has plenty of examples of massive strategic failures. Usually the armies failed because they were victorious earlier, and thus decided they had figured how to win now and into the future. There's nothing more seductive than victory on the battlefield for commanders and their staffs.

For the Japanese military leadership preparing for World War II in the late 1930s, they had only known victory across the Far East for decades. They had defeated huge military powers such as Russia and China in the early 1900s, on land, sea, and air. Full of hubris and tactical focus, they ignored effective strategic planning. Essentially, like the famous parable by Hans Christian Andersen, the Emperor's Generals and Admirals "were wearing no clothes" by the late 1930s. They conducted planning exercises designed to insure that, when they attacked the United States and others, victory was certain. And even when their deliberate planning exercises indicated a high probability of losing because their plans were flawed, they just changed the rules until the plans worked. Complacency proved fatal for the Japanese Empire in World War II.

Keeping the Cows Healthy and Content All Year Round

Next, we'll talk about the specifics of the 6 Core Strategic Values and Key Result Areas that underpin the Roadmap options, and how you can interpret them for your leadership in the Strategic Planning Process.

How do you take good care of your most valuable assets? As we've discussed, your key people and your intellectual property are your "sacred cows." You should spend the bulk of your time in the care and feeding of them, the critical components of your organization. Seems obvious, doesn't it?

Discipline and Experience Unleash Potential

For military leaders, everything centers on readiness. In the Army, we like saying "the best form of welfare for the troops is first class training." Our mission is to fight and win the Nation's wars. Military leaders have a very clear focus: train as you expect to fight, and build your strategic plans to support that focus. Some might think this creates a very rigid approach to strategic planning – but in fact, the opposite is true. Military leaders are trained to seize the initiative and challenge the accepted way of doing things, at every level.

For an Army officer, his or her strategic training occurs over years of progressive development. From the junior Lieutenant to the most senior Generals, we are trained to learn at one level, then go into the field for practical application, then back into the academic world, then back into the field. It's a very staircase-like process. The Army makes an extraordinary investment in leaders at every stage of development, so that officers understand strategic planning and execution at their requisite level of responsibility.

You probably don't have the luxury of the US military's commitment to years of first class leader training on strategic planning at increasingly complex levels. But you do have the ability to structure your process so that it is both efficient and effective, through the use of our 6 *Core Strategic Values (CPVs we will call them) or the application of Key Result Areas as they apply to your organization.* As you'll recall from the Roadmap, they form the left side of the matrix.

But these matrix entries are abbreviated versions of the CPVs. Here is a more detailed description of each one:

CPV1: Provide World Class Service: Of all the things you do, providing world class service is the bedrock of your company's value proposition. In the strategic planning process, you have to identify and measure the indicators of your service to your customers, your staff, and those who have the potential to become either one. Developing meaningful feedback is a critical measurement tool for how effectively you are providing that level of service.

CPV2: Develop and Maintain Rewarding Strategic Human Resources Systems: Your HR system should be far more than a set of procedures for your staff to follow. We have found that the best companies have very aggressive human resources systems – recruiting, training, rewarding, and succession planning. Just as with the other key components of your company (the sacred cows), some paranoia here is healthy. Demand performance outcomes. Promote from within as much as possible, track the retention rates of your staff, and include exit surveys and interviews to see where you failed to retain some key staff. Identify and resource a broad array of awards and recognition methods. Delegate authority to junior leaders to make HR decisions, such as awarding a spontaneous day off for an employee who steps up and accomplishes a difficult task on his or her own initiative.

CPV3: Establish and Exploit Self-Determined Opportunities: Define where you want to go. Everyone to some degree is a marketer in your company; the challenge is to identify where the meaningful opportunities are, resource them, and measure outcomes. One effective method we have seen used is to quantify business development opportunities. If you are going to pursue 4 new lines of business in the next 3 years, for example, have your Marketing Director conduct a formal study of each opportunity and where the ROI (Return on Investment) point is. Otherwise, you may fall victim to a whole bunch of the proverbial "good ideas" as a result of brainstorming sessions in the strategic planning session that don't go anywhere. Set delivery dates for these studies by your marketing team, and make sure the teams are interdisciplinary; that is, they are made up of people from all departments.

CPV4: Integrate Technology to Optimize Efficiency and Effectiveness: This is another area where the "good idea fairy" can run amok in the planning process without some numbers and planning discipline put into the process. That said, technology is also an area where true innovation and out of the box thinking can have a stunning impact on your bottom line. We recommend you approach this CPV without being tied to hardware or software as the discussion points; rather, look at what *key processes* you must follow and the *essential tasks* you must perform. Let them drive the strategic outcomes you're looking for. For example, if one of your key processes is to insure payroll is tracked and paid to your staff in a timely manner, then you should study the cost of performing that task in your current workforce and set a cost reduction goal (say 10% in the next 12 months). Using a time study, you can identify where the most expensive steps in the process are. Usually, that process is held hostage to the employee entries on some form of timesheet. The 10% cost reduction, then, is somewhere lurking inside that employee entry step. So, the answer lies in better technology to record those entries. Now you can focus the imagination of your team to find a technology solution, and put it into your CPV for one or more of your departments or business units.

CPV5: Establish and Maintain Financial Strength: This principle may seem to be the most obvious, but it is also the most difficult. Companies have an overwhelming tendency to spend what they have and then some, and count on growth to make up the difference. That's not using sound strategic planning as a method…..it's using hope. As one of our mentors once told us, "Hope is NOT a method." You have to set firm minimum standards for the amount of cash you will retain on hand, and develop measurable goals to insure that minimum grows as the company grows. Usually, the difference between the top line and bottom line offers excellent opportunity to find solutions for additional financial strength. Set goals inside the company to harvest money. Hold the leaders accountable for those goals as part of the strategic plan and their individual performance plans. It works.

CPV6: Identify and Maximize Key Strategic Relationships: Often cited at strategic planning sessions but rarely understood or implemented, innovative strategic partnerships can transform your company. For many leaders, though, the challenge of finding these relationships is daunting. And the issue of control always limits the effort. No one wants to lose control. Yet, these relationships with other companies can also limit much of your risk. Challenge your leaders to set goals for finding capabilities outside your company where you can save time, money, and still control the core elements of your organization. It doesn't have to be an all or nothing proposition.

If you elect to go the Key Result Area (KRA) approach, your strategic planning team will brainstorm what they need to be for your company and circumstances. KRAs are situationally dependent.

The example you'll find on our website at

www.LevelFiveAssociates.com/resources

is illustrative and lists the actual KRAs for a manufacturing company, to include

- **Achieve Marketing Excellence;**

- Nuclear Certification;

- Improve Profitability with a specific activity based costing model;

- Build a Team-centric, Performance based Culture;

- Streamline Customer Onboarding Process; and

- Launch a Partnership with a Key Customer.

Thoughts on Farming

We've used the dairy farm analogy in this handbook because it's important to consider your role as a leader in the strategic planning process – you are the "farmer" as steward of your company's future. Level Five leaders focus on the success of the organization, not themselves. Jim Collins' tremendous book, *Good to Great*, captured that quality through years of careful study of which companies built a framework for enduring market leadership. Even he admits he did not begin the study with the idea that there were such leaders. In fact, he admits it was a surprise:

"So, early in the project, I kept insisting, 'Ignore the executives.' But the research team kept pushing back……The good to great executives were all cut from the same cloth….All the good to great companies had Level 5 leadership." (Jim Collins: *Good to Great*, Collins Publishers, 2001, p.22)

They were simply great "farmers"….they grew leaders who understand the importance of focusing all of their energies on establishing and reinforcing the mission, vision/intent, and values through strategic planning and execution. They literally "walked the talk."

The Numbers Don't Lie

It's an established fact that companies which invest in strategic planning and the corollary leader development programs are four times more likely to be

successful than those that don't. That number should speak for itself. But it takes courage to change.

You have to move beyond that shortsightedness if you really want to be a Level Five Leader and turn the battleship that is your company. It does take time, energy, and preparation to lead strategically. However, the bottom line results and long term excellence you establish and maintain will create a legacy that will far outlast you. It can't be about you; it must be about the organization. And you must commit to the process for more than one rotation. Three years is the planning window for the Strategic Planning System for a good reason – it takes that long to change. Your Roadmap must not be a "one trick pony" that you schedule, execute, then proceed to ignore after the first planning session is over and you have checked that block.

The cycle starts with a careful review of who you are, what you do, and what your values are. Your leadership team has to participate in this critical stage of your strategic plan. Insist on the C-suite leaders being active members of this review. If they don't seem to have time to attend because of their busy travel schedules and similar excuses, you'll know they are not buying in to the importance of this process. You must make it clear they don't have anything better to do, and if they don't respond, then they are in the <u>wrong</u> seat on the <u>wrong</u> bus. Make the hard choice, and move them out.

Once you've established (or reestablished) your mission, vision/intent, and shared values, the Roadmap process will have traction. Follow through. Assign your best and brightest to help build the two-day strategic planning session, and require your senior executives to be there, too. Each of the CPVs or KRAs you establish must have measurable outcomes. Require your senior leaders and Business Unit Leaders to have management plans with timelines and milestones. Follow through with the periodic reviews. Level Five leaders hold people accountable. Your team will respect that disciplined approach.

When we served as Army officers in South Korea a few decades ago, the Army had a very short rotation cycle – 1 year – for every person assigned. The result was constant turmoil. Soldiers and leaders came into and out of units every month; it was extremely difficult to build cohesive teams. We had a saying that, "Anything you do in Korea more than 2 times becomes folklore", because if we could force our strategic planning process to remain consistent with that kind of turnover, we knew the newcomers would come into, and accept, an established process. Senior leaders insisted we remain disciplined and consistent. It paid off in our bottom line: combat readiness prevented war. The North Koreans knew we were a disciplined force, ready to fight and win if needed. They respected our readiness. The process worked.

You have your own challenges, hopefully without the severe personnel turbulence of the Army in South Korea during those years. The "folklore" established through creating and implementing a consistent Strategic Planning Process will grow a culture of excellence in your company. Innovation, profitability, and bottom line profits will all cascade from that culture, led by a team of fiercely loyal Level Five leaders. You'll establish the enduring foundation for change that will be there long after your watch.   So……Go for it!

About the Authors

Investing in leader development is the best investment you can make in your future. Level Five Associates represents over 80 years of military, corporate, and non-profit senior leadership experience. We are Army Major Generals, who have commanded Divisions, and we're also company presidents and CEOs of for profit and non-profit companies. As such, we offer unparalleled practical leadership experience, that's been honed in the laboratories of the Army and business.

> *"Experience is a prerequisite to progress! Nearly nine years ago I experienced progress as a friend of MG Robert Mixon. He led me to join the volunteer corps at Ft Carson, Co. His guidance and leadership led me to become a Good Neighbor at the Fort. Additionally, his abilities created a friendship for the post and the City of Pueblo which continues to thrive and grow. Prior to his command this condition did not exist."*
>
> *~ Marv Stein*

Whether large or small, every organization must grow and retain leaders to remain relevant. Once you know and understand the **Big 6 Leadership Principles™**, you'll see immediate results applying them in your organization. Partnering with Level Five Associates is like having your own "Leadership Board of Advisors." As leaders in the armed services and non-profit and for profit businesses, we get it!

Major General John Batiste
United States Army (retired)

John Batiste retired from active duty in November 2005 after more than 31 years of commissioned service. His final position in the Army was commanding general of the 1st Infantry Division, the "Big Red One", from August 2002-June 2005.

As an infantry officer, John served in a number of command and staff positions in peace, peace enforcement, and war. His command positions included E Company, 1-7 Cavalry, 1st Cavalry Division, Fort Hood, Texas; 3rd Battalion, 15th Infantry Regiment, 24th Infantry Division, Fort Stewart, Georgia; 2nd Brigade, 1st Armored Division, Baumholder, Germany (deployed to Bosnia-Herzegovina during the IFOR mission); and the 1st Infantry Division, Wurzburg, Germany (deployed to Kosovo, Turkey, and later Iraq during Operation Iraqi Freedom II).

His staff assignments included Executive Officer to the Assistant Commandant, US Army Infantry School and Brigade S3, 197th Infantry Brigade, Fort Benning, Georgia (deployed to the 1st Gulf War with the 24th Infantry Division); G3, 3rd Infantry Division, Wurzburg, Germany; and Deputy Director of Joint Warfighting Capabilities Assessment, J8, The Joint Staff and Senior Military Assistant to the Deputy Secretary of Defense, The Pentagon.

A 1974 graduate of the United States Military Academy, John earned a master's degree in financial management from the Naval Postgraduate School in Monterey, California (1981). He graduated from the Army War

College (1994), the Command and General Staff College (1986), and the Infantry Officer Advanced and Basic Courses (1975 and 1979, respectively).

After retirement from the Army, John shifted his attention to the for-profit corporate world and served as the president and CEO of Klein Steel Service Inc from 2005 to 2013, and the president and CEO of Buffalo Armory LLC from 2012 to the present. He is a past member of the executive committee and board of directors of the Metals Service Center Institute and the executive committee of Raffles Insurance Ltd. In support of veterans and their families, he serves as president of Stand for the Troops, is a board member of the Rochester-based Veterans Outreach Center, is a past and founding president of the Rochester Regional Veterans Business Council, and is a member of the board of advisors of the First Division Museum at Cantigny of Wheaton, Illinois.

John and his wife Michelle live in Brighton, New York and have five children and three grandchildren.

Major General Robert W. Mixon
United States Army (retired)

Major General (Ret) Robert W. Mixon, Jr., retired from active duty on October 1, 2007, after more than 33 years of commissioned service. At the time of his retirement he was Commanding General Division West, First Army and Fort Carson Colorado, having previously commanded the 7th Infantry Division.

Robert was an Armor Officer who served in command and staff positions throughout the Army in the United States and overseas. His command assignments include: Command of L Troop, 3rd Squadron, 11th Armored Cavalry Regiment at Bad Hersfeld, Germany; Command of 2nd Squadron, 3rd Armored Cavalry Regiment, Fort Bliss, Texas; Command of 1st Brigade, 2nd Infantry Division, Republic of Korea; and Commanding General, 7th Infantry Division, Fort Carson, Colorado.

He also served in several operations, plans, and training staff assignments, including: Deputy Executive Assistant to General Colin Powell, the Chairman of the Joint Chiefs of Staff, and Aide de Camp to General Crosbie Saint, Commander of U.S. Army Europe.

A 1974 graduate of the United States Military Academy, Major General Mixon also holds a Masters of Arts in History from Rice University. He is a distinguished graduate of the National War College (1996), School of Advanced Military Studies (1987), Command and General Staff College (1986), USMC Amphibious Warfare School (1980), Ranger School (1974), and the Armor Officer Basic Course (1974). He has also served at West Point as an Assistant Professor of History (1982-85).

After retirement from the Army, Robert was named President of Magnatag® Visible Systems in the fall of 2007. In September 2009 , he became Executive Vice President of Unistel, the employee services company of CDS Monarch, a nonprofit for the developmentally disabled in Rochester, New York. Since that time, CDS Monarch has begun a pioneering program, Warrior

Salute, for Veterans with Traumatic Brain Injury and PTSD.

Robert and his West Point classmate, Major General (retired) John Batiste founded their leadership company, Level Five Associates, LLC, in 2009. Level Five provides companies, organizations, and individuals with dynamic leadership presentations and tailored, outcomes based leader development programs and strategic planning services.

Robert and his wife Ruth live in Pittsford, New York, and have two sons. Both serve on active duty in the United States Army. Robert has served on the Governor's Commission on Veterans' Affairs, the Board of Directors of the Veteran's Outreach Center in Rochester, New York, and on the Veteran's Business Council. He is also President of the West Point Class of 1974.

Made in the USA
Columbia, SC
06 February 2020